BEAR LIBRARY
BEAR, DE 19701

06/11/1998

BEAR LIBRARY
BEAR, DE 19701

HISTORIC
COMMUNITIES

The Kitchen

Bobbie Kalman

Crabtree Publishing Company

HISTORIC COMMUNITIES

Created by Bobbie Kalman

For Beryl Tupman's
grade six class

Editors
Marni Hoovegeen
Christine Arthurs

Design
Heather Delfino

Pasteup
Adriana Longo

Published by
Crabtree Publishing Company

350 Fifth Avenue	360 York Road, RR 4	73 Lime Walk
Suite 3308	Niagara-on-the-Lake	Headington
New York	Ontario, Canada	Oxford OX3 7AD
N.Y. 10118	L0S 1J0	United Kingdom

Copyright © **1990, 1993 CRABTREE PUBLISHING COMPANY**. All rights reserved. No part of this publication may be reproduced, stored in a retrieval system or be transmitted in any form or by any means, electronic, mechanical, photocopying, recording, or otherwise, without the prior written permission of Crabtree Publishing Company.

Cataloguing in Publication Data

Kalman, Bobbie, 1947-
 The kitchen

(Historic communities)
ISBN 0-86505-484-3 (library bound) ISBN 0-86505-504-1 (pbk.)
This book takes a close look at a pioneer kitchen and examines the utensils used. Cooking, making bread and butter, and preserving food are among the topics discussed.

1. Kitchen utensils - Juvenile literature. 2. Cookery - History - Juvenile literature. 3. Frontier and pioneer life - Juvenile literature. I. Title. II. Series: Kalman, Bobbie, 1947- . Historic communities.

TX653.K33 1990   j643'.3'097   LC 93-6207

Contents

The heart of the home

If you could travel back in time to visit a kitchen of long ago, you would find it to be quite different from your kitchen at home. The first thing you would notice is that many of the things you are used to seeing in modern kitchens are missing. Stoves, refrigerators, dishwashers, and microwave ovens all need electricity, and electricity was not yet invented.

There were no lamps to switch on to make the room extra bright. Sunlight coming through the window lit the kitchen during the day. At night, the room was dark except for the glow of the fire and a candle or two.

Compare the two kitchens shown above. Pick out what is different in each one. What activities take place in the kitchens? What makes each one a pleasant place to be?

Plain and simple

The settler kitchen was not fancy. The walls were bare, and the windows were small, but the dancing flames in the fireplace made the room feel cosy and cheerful. The whole family liked to gather here. The kitchen was the heart of the settler home.

Visiting a kitchen from the past

Thanks to many people who take an interest in the past, you do not have to travel back in time to see a kitchen of yesterday. You can visit one in an historic house or community near you and observe how the settlers cooked their meals, did their chores, and enjoyed themselves in their busy kitchens.

When you visit historic communities, you may see kitchens from different time periods. Some belonged to the very early settlers, and some to settlers from a later time. None of them had electricity or modern plumbing.

The most important room

In many of the homes first built by the settlers, the kitchen was the only room in the house. This all-purpose room had a dirt floor and only a few pieces of furniture, which were usually handmade. Rough planks placed over saw-horses served as the kitchen table. Instead of chairs, early kitchens had benches or stools. Sometimes there was not enough sitting space, so the children had to stand while they ate.

In these early homes, kitchens were used for sleeping as well as cooking. Beds were sometimes built right into the walls. Some settlers slept on turn-up beds that could be hooked up onto the wall when not in use, and others had beds that were used as benches during the day.

The early settlers slept in their kitchens. Notice the cradle and daybed against the right wall.

In later times, settler homes were much larger and had several bedrooms. The kitchen was a separate room that was used for cooking, eating, and as a gathering place. Cupboards and shelves were added for storing dishes and kitchen gadgets. The floors were made from wooden planks.

The center of activity

The kitchen was the center of family activity. Spinning, weaving, and making candles were just a few of the jobs that were carried out there. Children helped prepare the meals, learned sewing and carving, and read by the fire. Although men usually worked outdoors during the day, they joined the rest of the family by the fire in the evening, where everyone read books and letters, sang songs, told stories, and enjoyed one another's company.

Families liked to gather together for hearty evening meals (bottom). They also enjoyed reading to one another by firelight (top).

Welcome to a settler kitchen!

8

Keeping the fire lit

The first fireplaces were so large that seats were built right into the sides of the chimney. On cold winter evenings, the settlers huddled close to the flames in order to stay warm.

The settlers spent much of their time in front of the kitchen fireplace. Besides being the only source of heat, it was also the source of light for sewing and reading.

Burning night and day

The settlers kept a huge log burning night and day. Overnight, the fire died down to just a few hot coals. In the morning, an early riser brought the fire back to life by adding **kindling** and logs to the coals. The settlers were careful not to let the fire go out because starting another one was a difficult job. The settlers had no matches in the early days.

Starting a new fire

When a fire went out, the easiest way to start a new one was to use a flint and **tinderbox**. A flint was used to make a spark. The hard way of lighting a fire was to go to a neighbor's house and borrow some burning coal. The child who performed this chore ran home carrying the coal in the bottom of a metal pail.

(left) The fire was kept burning all the time because it was needed for cooking and keeping warm.

(right) Someone had to cut down the trees, chop firewood from logs, and stack it up in the woodshed.

Cooking over the fire

There are many kinds of pots and pans in your kitchen. Some of them are used in the oven, and others are for your stovetop. The early settlers did not have the choice in cookware that we have today. Most of their pots and **utensils** were made of iron. They were all meant to be used in a fireplace.

Long handles

The handles of your pots, pans, and cooking utensils are made from a special material that does not get hot. The settlers did not have handles like this. Instead, they made the handles of their fireplace utensils very long. Long utensils did not get hot at the ends because it took much longer for heat to travel along the handles. They also allowed the cook to stay at a safe distance from the fire as she stirred the food.

Skillets with legs

The bed of coals at the bottom of a fireplace was used for frying eggs, pancakes, fish, and meat. The settlers could not put their pots and pans directly onto the coals because the fire would be smothered. The coals needed air to keep burning. In order to keep the skillets and pots raised above the coals, some of them were made with legs. When they did not have legs, they were placed on stands with legs called **trivets**.

*(opposite) Long-handled frying pans with legs were called **spiders**. Does this one look like a spider to you?*

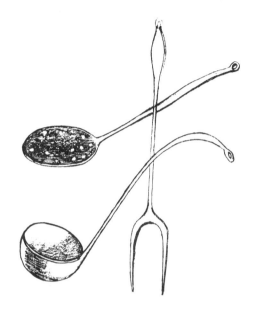

Many of the settlers' pots had legs to keep them standing above the coals.

Above the flames

Much of the food made by the settlers was cooked in heavy iron pots. Meat and vegetables were put in these pots and boiled together to produce hearty soups and stews. These one-pot meals simmered all day, hanging on a pole over the fire.

From lugpole to crane

The first type of pole used for hanging pots was called a **lugpole**. It was made from moist, green wood. If the lugpole was not replaced regularly, it dried out and broke, usually while a pot was hanging from it. The whole meal would then spill into the flames.

The later settlers who had blacksmiths in their areas had **cranes** made for their fireplaces. The crane was anchored into the side of the fireplace. It swung in and out of the fireplace, allowing the cook to stir the food without having to come too close to the fire.

Roasting meat

Large pieces of meat were roasted over the fire. The early settlers simply hung the roast up on a rope. In later days, settlers used **jacks** to turn their meat so it would cook on all sides. One type of jack, a **clock jack**, was a small gadget with a hook at its bottom. The roast was put onto this hook, and the jack was wound up like a clock. It turned the roast around and around while the cook prepared the rest of the meal. (See page 8)

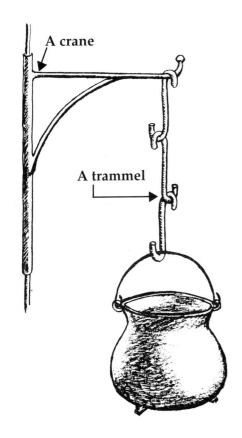

A crane

A trammel

The kettles and pots that hung over the fire were attached to a crane with hooks. A system of hooks that could raise and lower the pots over a fire was called a **trammel.** *When the stew boiled, the cook could remove a hook from the trammel and move the pot farther up from the flame.*

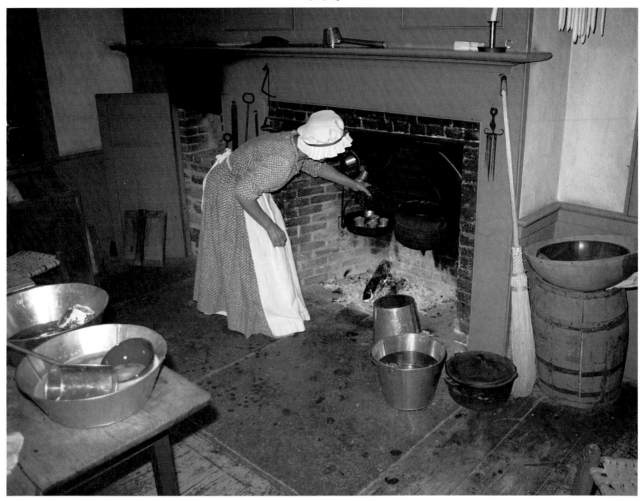

(above) A Dutch oven was a big pot used for baking bread, rolls, biscuits, and shortcake. It was placed among the hot coals, and more coals were heaped on top. Can you spot a Dutch oven in this picture? It is right next to the broom.

(left) Meat was often roasted on a **spit**. Meat on the spit was cooked right over the flames or in a metal box called a **roasting kitchen**. *The open side of the box faced the fire, and the box trapped the heat. A small door allowed the cook to baste the roast.*

Ovens and stoves

I n some historic kitchens, you might see special **bread ovens** that were built right into the side of brick fireplaces. To bake bread, the bread oven was first filled with hot coals, which heated the bricks. The coals turned to ashes and were swept out. When the oven cooled down a bit, it was ready for baking. The bread was placed in the oven on a long-handled, flat shovel called a **peel**. The heat of the bricks baked the bread.

Some homes had two bread ovens. One was beside the fireplace, and the other was outdoors. The indoor one was used in winter and the outdoor one in summer.

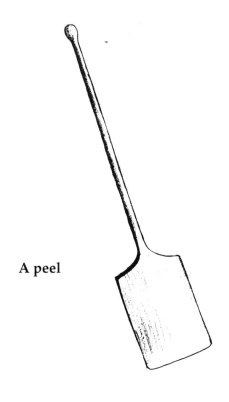

A peel

The bread oven was built for baking bread, cookies, cakes, and biscuits. Because this one was indoors, it helped heat the home in winter. In summer, some settlers used outdoor bread ovens so their homes would not become too hot.

A better way to cook

Later homes had stoves instead of fireplaces. A stove was made of iron, and the fire was built right inside. At first, much of the smoke stayed in the kitchen because there was no pipe to take it out. Later models used a system of pipes to direct the smoke up through the chimney.

Stoves were much better than fireplaces for both heating and cooking. The heat of the stove stayed in the room, whereas much of the heat in the fireplace was lost up the chimney. Smaller and lighter pots could be used with stoves, making cooking less of a chore. The later stoves also had built-in water heaters and ovens for baking bread and rolls.

water heater

oven

This settler girl churns butter in her summer kitchen. Stoves were moved into summer kitchens to keep the rest of the house cooler. In winter, summer kitchens were used for storage. Food stayed cold because the room was no longer heated by the stove.

Plenty of food

We know how the settlers cooked their food, but where did they get it? There were no grocery stores or supermarkets in the early days. Fortunately for the settlers, food was all around them. They hunted and trapped animals and birds, caught fish in rivers and lakes, and gathered fruit from the forests. They also grew their own fruits, vegetables, and grain, and raised farm animals such as cows, pigs, goats, turkeys, and chickens.

To replace white sugar, the settlers made sugar and syrup from the sap of maple trees. They grew herbs to make their food taste better.

Herbs and spices

Many of the early settlers brought seeds of herbs such as thyme, sage, marjoram, rosemary, and dill with them from their former homes. They planted the seeds in their gardens to grow herbs for seasoning food. Herbs added tasty flavors to stews and meats. Some herbs were also used as medicine. They were boiled or dried, crushed, and mixed to form pastes. The Native People sometimes showed the settlers how to use the herbs, roots, and berries that grew in the forests.

Discovering new foods

Some foods and spices, such as sugar, coffee, tea, cinnamon, and cloves, were not available to the settlers. These products only grew in warm climates. The settlers, however, found ways to replace some of these things. For instance, they discovered how to make a sweet syrup from the sap of the maple tree. They also made a coffee-like beverage from dandelions and tea from raspberry roots and leaves.

(right) Kneading bread dough was tough work. Bread makers needed strong muscles to prepare it for baking.

The settlers who had no gristmill nearby had to grind grain themselves. They crushed it into a coarse flour using a mortar and pestle (top), but this took a long time and was very hard work. Some settlers owned **querns,** (above) which ground the grain between two heavy stones. The bottom stone stayed still while the top one was turned by hand.

Homemade bread

Everyone loves the smell of bread baking in the oven. It is so wonderful, it makes your mouth water. Have you ever thought about the difficulties the settlers must have had putting bread on their tables?

Flour from grain

The main ingredient in bread is flour, which comes from grain. Many kinds of grain can be used to make bread. Some of these are wheat, corn, rye, and oats. Before the settlers could make bread, however, they first had to grind the grain into flour. This was not easy to do because all grains have protective shells, which are hard to crush.

More hard work

Once the grain was ground into flour, the work of baking bread began. But bread is not just flour! You need other ingredients, too. These are milk, water, yeast, lard, salt, and sugar. A settler had to milk a cow, kill a pig, and fetch water in order to have these ingredients. Someone also had to chop wood to make a fire in the bread oven.

When people settled in an area that had a gristmill, they could take their grain to the miller and have him grind it into flour. Sometimes the settlers had to travel two or three days to reach the nearest mill. After traveling this long distance, they must have enjoyed biting into a slice of freshly baked bread.

Make a design on the top of your butter with an old butter stamp such as this one.

(right) Buttermilk is the liquid that is left over after butter is churned. A woman pours it off to save as a refreshing drink.

A butter churn could be a stone crock or a thin, wooden barrel. The dasher was pumped up and down through a hole in the top. The settlers made sure the churn was spotless because butter takes on the taste and smell of its container.

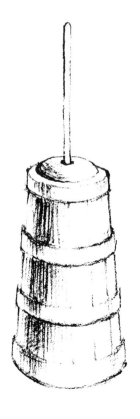

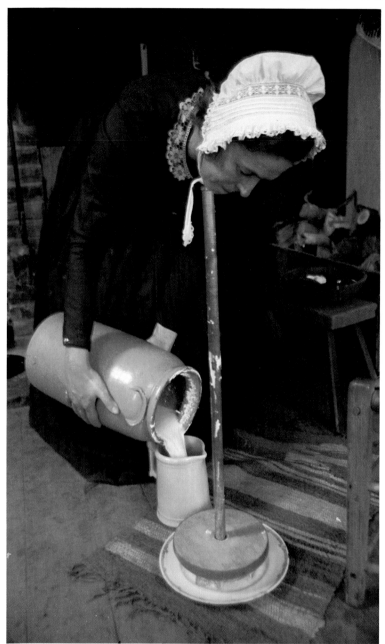

Making butter

Settler families kept at least one dairy cow so they would have milk to drink and butter to put on bread. Someone milked the cow each day, and part of the milk was set aside for making butter. It was placed in a stone crock and kept in a cool room for a day or two. The creamy portion of the milk, which rose to the top, was skimmed off and put into a **butter churn**.

Beat it!

There are tiny particles of fat in cream. When these stick together, they form butter. This happens when the **dasher** in the churn is pumped up and down and rolled between the hands. These actions separate the butter particles from the liquid. Before too long, small clumps of butter start to form at the bottom of the churn. These pieces become bigger and start floating in the liquid. Then they are ready to be taken out, washed, and pressed into butter molds.

Make your own butter

You can make fresh butter in your own home or classroom. It is easy and fun. Warm a cup of whipping cream to room temperature and put it into a clean glass jar with a lid. Add a few well-washed marbles to the jar and replace the lid. Shake the jar without stopping until butter forms. The marbles work in the same way a dasher does in a churn. Pour off the buttermilk and rinse your butter with water.

(left) Fresh butter was washed with clean water to remove the last drops of buttermilk. The extra water was squeezed out with a wooden paddle.

(right) You can make fresh butter, too. To help you keep the beat while shaking the cream, chant this old rhyme:

> *Come, butter, come,*
> *Come, butter, come,*
> *Samantha's standing*
> * by the gate,*
> *Waiting for her butter cake,*
> *Come, butter, come.*

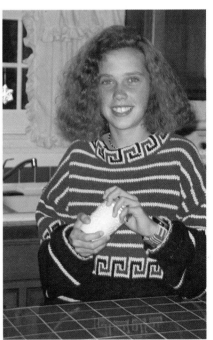

Wood and iron kitchen utensils

The early settlers carved their kitchen containers and utensils from wood. Their fireplace tools were made of iron.

The early settlers ate off wooden plates and drank from wooden cups.

The settlers needed many buckets, tubs, and barrels. They did not have plastic containers, so they used wood. This bucket with a long handle is called a **piggin**.

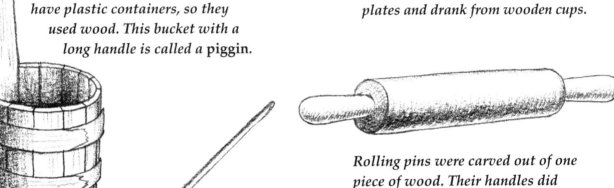

Rolling pins were carved out of one piece of wood. Their handles did not move as the handles of today's rolling pins do. What are rolling pins for?

The piggin and this long spoon were used with maple sap.

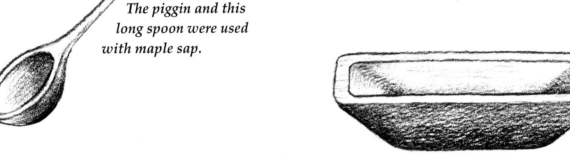

Wooden spoons were for scooping flour or apple butter.

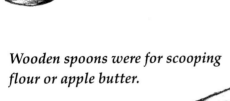

A wooden bowl such as this one was made from a log that was cut lengthwise and hollowed out. People used it for eating, mixing food, or displaying fruit and vegetables. These bowls were called canoes. "Canoe" guess why?

Bread was toasted over the fire in this old-fashioned iron toaster.

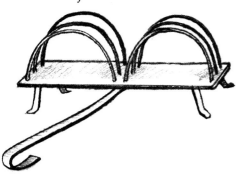

Potatoes were put inside this potato boiler, which was immersed in a huge pot of water. When the potatoes were cooked, it was lifted out of the pot, and the water drained away.

The crane was attached to the wall of the fireplace and swung in and out so the cook could reach the food more easily.

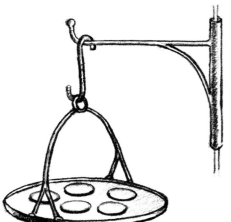

Many pans and utensils that were used for fireplace cooking had long handles to keep the cook away from the heat, and the heat away from the cook's hand.

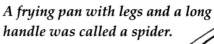

A kettle of water hung over the fire all day long. The hot water was used to make tea and coffee, wash dishes and clothes, and for bathing. There were no taps from which settlers could get hot water.

A frying pan with legs and a long handle was called a spider.

(above) Dried apples were a favorite winter treat. Herbs and corn (below) were also hung from the ceiling to dry by the heat of the fire. These dried foods could be stored and eaten later, providing the settlers with vitamins long after the harvest.

Preserving food

We keep our food from spoiling by storing it in our refrigerators or freezers. The settlers had no refrigerators, but they had several ways of preserving their food.

Drying meat and fruit

The settlers kept meat and fish from going bad by drying it. Meat and fish were sliced into thin strips and laid out to dry in the sun for several days. When the dried strips were added to water and vegetables in a pot, the result was a delicious soup or stew. Fruit was also dried. For instance, apple slices were strung on pieces of string and hung by the fireplace. Herbs were also dried so they could be used in the winter months.

These two women make sauerkraut, which lasts much longer than cabbage.

Meat was hung inside the smokehouse (below) to give it extra flavor as well as preserve it. Hickory wood gave meat an especially good taste.

Keeping it cool

Vegetables were kept cool in underground **root cellars**. Other places for keeping food cold were springs, rivers, and wells. Some settlers built special **ice houses**. In winter, big chunks of ice were cut from a river or lake and put into a big hole in the floor of the ice house. The ice was packed with straw and sawdust to keep it from melting. It kept the small building cool.

Smoking and pickling

Settlers also salted, smoked, and pickled their food to preserve it. Vegetables such as cucumbers, onions, and cabbages were pickled. Pickled meat was packed in a barrel. Some types of meat were preserved in a smoke house. Ham and bacon are examples of smoked meats.

(above) These two girls must wash the dinner dishes without a kitchen sink. Instead, they heat water on the fire and soak the dishes in the wash tub. They do not use any soap. The water, which contains the leftover food from the plates, is then given to the animals as a nutritious drink.

(right) Water was often a fair distance from the house in a river, lake, or well. How many trips would you have to make before you had enough water for a bath?

Kitchen facts

If you cannot find a watertap or a garbage can on your visit, do not be surprised. The settlers had to bring in their water from a well or from a nearby stream. There was no garbage because they threw very little away. Scraps of food were given to animals, fat was used to make soap and candles, and old clothes were cut up to make quilts or rugs. Almost everything was reused in one way or another.

(top, left) One day every week was called Wash Day. The children were sent for water, which was put on the fire to heat up early in the morning. The women of the home got out their soap, tubs, and scrubbing boards. Scrub, scrub, scrub. Every single piece of clothing had to be pounded and rubbed on the washing board until all the dirt was out.

(top, right) Everyone had chores to do in the settler home. Young children were often in charge of finding kindling, or small pieces of wood that were used to get fires going in the morning.

Without electric lamps, settlers had to provide their own light. They made candles by melting down animal fat. Reading by candlelight was hard on the eyes.

A family dinner

The later settlers had their grain ground at the mill and raised farm animals for food. They grew crops in their fields and herbs in their gardens. They enjoyed good meals compared to the early settlers who had to hunt and trap and grind their grain by hand.

The large settler family crowds around the table after a hard day's work, eager to enjoy the bountiful meal. Tonight is a special night because it is Uncle Luke's birthday. Mother and Aunt Rose spent the day preparing a feast in his honor. They have baked whole-wheat bread and churned butter from fresh, sweet cream. The first dish served is a vegetable broth that had simmered over the fire all afternoon. A chicken that was perfectly roasted on a spit is next, along with a tasty gravy, boiled potatoes, turnips, and fiddleheads. Everyone has generous helpings of food, including Max, the cat, who keeps begging for more. The highlight of the meal is Uncle Luke's birthday cake. His eyes light up when he sees it!

Glossary

bountiful - Plentiful

community - A group of people who live together in one area and share buildings, services, and a way of life. A community is also the place in which these people live.

crock - A pot or jar made of clay

early settler - A person who is among the first people to settle in an area. A settler from an early time in history. A pioneer

fiddlehead - The curled end of a young fern that is considered a delicacy

gadget - A small tool or unusual device

grain - A hard seed or kernel of a cereal plant

gristmill - A mill that grinds grain

herb - A plant used to flavor foods

historic - Important in history. Historic places are important because they teach us how the people who settled this continent lived in the past.

iron - A hard, black metal

kindling - Dry twigs or small pieces of wood used to start fires

lard - A white, greasy substance made by melting down pig fat

later settler - A settler who moved into an area in which other people already lived

Native People - A group of people who were born in an area and whose ancestors were the first to live in that region

plank - A thick, long board that was cut from a log

plumbing - A set of pipes and taps through which water flows

preserve - To keep food from spoiling

quern - A hand mill with two large stones used for grinding grain

root cellar - An underground cold room for storing fruits and vegetables

sawhorse - A triangular frame on which wood rests when it is being sawed

settler - A person who makes his or her home in a new country or part of a country that is not built up

skillet - A frying pan with a long handle

spider - A skillet with legs

summer kitchen - A kitchen that was built onto the outside of a home and was used in summer

tinderbox - A small metal box equipped with a flint and steel for making sparks

trammel - A system of hooks on which pots were hung in a fireplace

utensil - A tool or container used in making or doing something

whole wheat - Containing all three parts of a grain of wheat—the endosperm, germ, and bran

yeast - A substance used for baking bread. It makes bread rise.

Kitchen index

Acknowledgments

Photographs:
Marc Crabtree: p.20(right)
Metro Region Conservation Authority: p.5, 7(top and bottom), 11(left), 12, 16, 19(top and bottom), 20(bottom left), 21, 27(top), 28(left), 29(all three)
Environment Canada. Canadian Parks Service, Ontario Region: Cover, p.22, 26(top)
Niagara National Historic Site: p.28(right)
Jim Bryant: p.6, 15(bottom), 20(top left), 26(bottom)
Ken Faris: p.15(top)
Upper Canada Village-The St. Lawrence Parks Commission: Title page, p.17, 23(left), 27(bottom)
Bobbie Kalman: p.4, 23(right)
Bob Mansour: p.11(right), 13, 29(top right)

Illustrations:
Cover: Antoinette "Cookie" DeBiasi
Halina Below-Spada: p.8-9
John Mantha: p.10 (colorized etching)
National Archives/C-1118, Edmond J. Massicotte: p.30
David Willis: p.13, 14, 16, 22-23, 24-25
Janet Wilson: p.18

10 11 12 13 14 Printed in U.S.A. 9 8 7

J 643.3097 K   Kalman, Bobbie,

                 The kitchen.

$19.16   33910030868724
                 06/11/1998

BEAR LIBRARY
BEAR, DE 19701

06/11/1998